So You Want to Write a Book?

Advice To Jumpstart Your Publishing Success

Othniel J. Seiden

Boomer Book Series Publication

Cover Art
by Capri Brock
DesignsByCapri.com

BooomerBookSeries.com

ISBN: 1519496079

To Greg,
Eric
& Kurt

It is my goal
that you use this advice
to jumpstart
Your Publishing Success...

If I can write a publishable book,
so can you!

What are my qualifications as a writer?

Do I have an excellent background in college English, Literature and Creative Writing ... No!

Am I a whiz at grammar ...No!

Yet I have over 20 books published in spite of the above !

Why should you read this book?

You picked up this book because of the title. You must want to write a book. Maybe you already have a book started or even finished and are wondering what to do next.

This book is for you and for anyone else who wants to write a book, articles, short stories, a family history.

This book will be especially helpful to anyone in an industry that is in a "Publish or Perish" situation.

CONTENTS

"THEY" WERE WRONG!

When I first started writing over twenty-five years ago, I took several writing courses from various authors, English teachers, poets, literary agents and people in the publishing industry.

The one thing I remember is that they told me that getting published was *extremely difficult*. They also said that only *one in a hundred thousand would succeed*. Well, since then I've had well over twenty books published, and that was while I was practicing medicine full time and writing as an avocation.

Either I'm really beating the odds - or they were wrong!

> *I'm here to tell you,*
> *"They were wrong and*
> *that if I could do it*
> *almost anyone can do it".*

MY QUALIFICATIONS AS A WRITER

Do I have an excellent background in college English, Literature and Creative Writing? No!

Am I a whiz at grammar? No!

I doubt I ever earned better than a "C" in any English course I ever took in grade, high school or college, nor did I ever have much interest in literature or creative writing courses that I was *forced* to take. I certainly wouldn't have taken them as an elective.

Now please understand, I'm not bragging that I was a poor student. What I want you to understand is that if you really want to write a book, you can publish it and you can get it sold. I've been able to have over 20 books published in spite any perceived scholarly deficit.

WHO SHOULD READ THIS BOOK?

This book can help anyone who wants to write books, articles, short stories, family histories or trade articles. It can especially help anyone in academics or an industry that is in a "Publish or Perish" situation.

> ## *If you can speak,*
> ## *You can write!*

My philosophy is that, "if you can speak, you can write." If you have something to say and can express yourself in plain talk, there is no reason why you can't express yourself in writing. The secret to getting your writing published is finding the proper audience ... those readers interested in what you have to say ... and identifying the publishers who reach those readers. Believe me when I tell you this last step is more important that your writing ability, style and talent.

I'm living proof that writing is the most forgiving art form in the entire world!

I'll stick my neck out and assure you that if you read this book, or take one of my one day classes, or both, finish a manuscript and not just come up with a great title, and do what I suggest, you'll end up with a published product!

That's the best I can promise you.

BOOK IDEAS ARE EVERYWHERE

Think about what **you** are most interested in.

Write about your interests. It makes it more interesting to research. That's not to say that you can only write about things you've experienced; far from it. Were that myth true no one would ever write about the Civil War ever again. If you're interested in something or have specific needs, so do others. Look to your experiences for ideas. If you have experience or expertise in any subject, there are others who want to learn from you.

> *What do you know more about than most other people?*

Book ideas are everywhere! Learn to tune your self in to them. Change short stories to novels. Articles can lead to other articles or stories. You own the rights, so redress the same material into a new product. Plagiarize yourself, it will give your idea wider exposure and open new markets. If you've written a book and have done the research for it then consider if you can take chapters or parts out of it to sell as articles. Recycle!

If you read a short story or article and think it should be expanded into a book, go for it! What do you do in your "day job?" Consider making a self-help book out of it.

Once you tune in, writing projects will inundate you. You'll discover your problem won't be to find ideas, but to decide which ideas are worth pursuing or what priority they hold in your list of things to write. Chances are you already have an idea for a writing project, or you probably wouldn't be reading this book now. So let's examine how to determine if the idea is really worth developing further.

RESEARCHING YOUR IDEA

Look at your project as a product, not as a work of art. Your writing project is a product as much as if you were considering an invention ... say a better mouse trap ... a new kitchen gadget... or a product that will turn you car into a vehicle that gets 100 miles to the gallon. If you had an idea to produce and market any one of these items you would hopefully ask yourself some important questions before investing time and effort in pursuing the project.

Has it been done before?
It probably has and it is okay if the answer is yes!!!

There have been millions of books published over the past decades and there are few really new ideas out there. Pick almost any book you can think of and you'll probably find others that are at least similar. Take your idea and see what has been done on the subject in the past. You may find there are several books very closely related to your subject. Does that mean you should scrap your idea or project? Not at all! The fact that there are several competitors out there just means that the idea is probably a good one - timely, in demand. But it does mean you have to ask yourself a few more questions.

How will yours differ?

Once an idea catches in your brain, examine it from all angles. If it has been done, think about how you can improve it. How can you do it in another genre, to another audience? Don't dismiss any idea until you're sure it has no chance of success. There might be other reasons to scrap it, but this one is actually very unlikely.

Are there new developments since the last time those ideas were published? If there aren't new developments then there may well be new audiences for the project. If nothing else you may have a better way of expressing the idea.

> *Every year there are a million new people who've never seen an elephant!* ~*P.T. Barnum*

What's new?

What has changed since the last time this topic has been written about? Do the changes warrant another book? Look to see what the latest book on your topic had to say and determine if your viewpoint is different enough to get the attention and interest of your potential audience.

In 1981 I wrote one of the first, if not the first book on exercise walking, titled "Walk, the easy way to get in shape." A few years later I wrote another titled "HealthWalk." In those few years several other authors wrote walking books, but still there were enough studies and developments to warrant my doing another exercise walking book. If I decided today to do a third walking book I think I'd find a big enough audience to make it worthwhile. Keep in mind what P.T. Barnum said, *"Every year there are a million new people who've never seen an elephant!"* Markets change and grow constantly.

Get a feel for what your public wants.

There are a lot of potential readers who want to get into better fitness. They are limited for time. They are lazy. They don't want to spend a lot of money on personal trainers or have to join an expensive health club. They don't want to show off their out-of-shape pathetic body by having to work out in a gym full of jocks with six-pack abs. A book that tells them that exercise walking is one of the best exercises for human kind, can benefit them if done only 30 minutes a day three to five times a week, does not require expensive equipment, can be done out of sight of well developed beautiful people … such a book is bound to sell. Find out as much as is possible about your readers, then give them what they want!

Market Research

Now that you've decided that your idea is a good one, you need to research it further. You've looked at what your competition is, the other books on the same or similar subjects. Now it's time to research your potential readers.

Who are your readers?

The better you know your readers the better you can serve them. Are they limited to a specific sex, age group, financial level, religion, educational level, etc. etc. etc? I wrote a book in the 80's entitled, ***"Coping With Miscarriage."*** My main market was obviously women, though some husbands no doubt would have some interest in the book, the target market was still mostly women. They would be mainly of child bearing age and mainly those having had a miscarriage. Since one in four pregnancies end in miscarriage that is a sizable market. Miscarriage crosses all educational levels, religions and economic levels, so the book had to be written to be understood by all levels of education and not be disrespectful, demeaning or insulting to any religious beliefs or social levels.

Look at your book as a product!

Look at your book as a product

Don't think about your book as a work of art, but as a product. This is extremely important at this stage of preparation for your writing. How would you market research your invention? Do your market research as if you were inventing a "better mouse trap." The artsy aspect of your book will take care of itself in the writing.

Now you want to double check and market research to determine the market need.

Go to the internet, library, book store, Google, Amazon.com, BarnesAndNoble.com, etc. and recheck your competition. See what viewpoint the other books are taking. What is their purpose? You don't have to read the books, but scan their introductions, tables of contents and indexes to get a feel for what they are about. Then consider how you want to tailor your book to make it more distinctive, comprehensive, memorable or important to your target readership.

TARGET YOUR MARKET

We've already briefly touched on knowing your readers, but it's important enough to give them a chapter of their own.

You wouldn't want to invent a new type lock pick without knowing who wanted to pick locks. Are they mostly crooks, police, people locked out of their own homes, how many crooks are there, how many cops, how many home owners, etc., etc, etc. Authors should give the same consideration to their readers and as you'll see later, this knowledge will be more important to selling your book to a publisher or agent than your writing ability!

Who will be interested?

Years ago I wrote a book entitled, ***"Coping With Your Bad Back."*** So who would be interested in that? Anyone with back pain was the simple answer. But simple answers aren't enough. To really know your potential readers and write your book to get the maximum percentage of that potential market you want to get more specific. Knowing the details about that market will really define the purpose of your book and also help you sell your book. So let's look into these important details.

Who is your target market?

We've already decided anyone with a bad back or just

occasional back pain is interested in this material, that's almost a given. But how can we expand that audience? What about the people who treat back pain? Should I write the book to be of interest to just the sufferers of back pain or can I expand the market to their caregivers - people with whom I share the market? Professionals like chiropractors, doctors, nurses, acupuncturists, massage therapists, physical therapists, personal trainers and other healthcare workers all need to know this information too. Is there enough new information to interest these "fringe" readers? Should I write this book so it will interest these professionals (i.e. be understandable to specifically trained caregivers or to less specifically educated back pain patients?) Maybe there is a market for two books, one aimed at a professional market and one aimed at a patient market. Always think with an open mind and be willing to "write" outside the box.

How many are they?

When I wrote *"Coping With Your Bad Back,"* I discovered that every morning 80,000 people woke up each morning saying, "Oh my aching back!" That's a huge potential market. I liked that number, and more important my publisher *loved* that number. That number had more to do with the selling of the book to the publisher than did my writing skills. At that time, I didn't even think about the fringe market potential. Now that I'm more experienced, I think I may want to rewrite or write a new book on coping with back pains considering the fringe market, the patient market and all the developments in back treatment since I wrote the first book. Try to get the best statistics on who your readers are and how many readers your potential market includes.

What are they like?

What are the people with bad backs or occasional back pain like? For one thing, they come from all walks of life. The fact is even the professionals who make up the fringe audience for the book get sore backs at least occasionally. Bad backs happen to the unfit and the very fit as well. People who work out a lot get occasional acute back strains and often chronic back problems. The unfit will often get the same acute or chronic pains. Men and women are probably equally cursed with back afflictions. Mothers with young children are frequently victims of back disorders from picking up their young children. Children on the other hand are rarely cursed with back pain. Rich or poor alike are potential readers. Race, religion or ethnicity has little bearing on back problems, but age is definitely a factor.

What are their reading habits and levels?

Reading level of your potential readers is of great importance. You don't want to write down to your public nor do you want to get so technical that only professionals can understand you. With such diversity as a book on back disorders has, you have to select a reading level that is fairly simple. I selected to write Coping With Your Bad Back at about a third grade level. That may sound fairly elementary to you, however that is the level that most news papers are written to.

> *The fine line you have to walk is that you need to be perceived as an expert without seeming arrogant or condescending.*

Write as you would speak conversationally. Use lots of examples to describe and emphasize the points you are making. You also need to tread another narrow line so that you don't bore or insult your more professional and college educated readers.

Now that you've done your market and readership research, decide if your project still is a good idea? If so, go for it. If not, what changes can I make to improve the idea and the market? Is it worth that effort? Sleep on it if you must before you throw out the idea if you have doubts. If you put it out of your mind for a day or two a light may go on and an idea may pop into your head that makes it more feasible, or it may lead to a completely new idea that works better for you. Having insight to the market you've been studying may suggest a new project to you which is of interest. Never be too quick to throw out ideas. Something made you think it a good idea in the beginning. It may just require a different slant to make it change from questionable to great. Be open to inspiration!

CHOOSE THE BEST GENRE

Will this idea work as a novel, a self-help, a history, an e-book, an audio book, a teleseminar or all of the above?

Some years ago I wrote a book entitled, *"The Capuchin."* It is a historical fiction about the life of Padre Pio, a Capuchin monk who died in 1968 and who has already been granted sainthood by the Vatican. Padre Pio was a mystic and a miracle worker who bore the Stigmata or the wounds of Jesus which would bleed from time to time from the sites where Jesus was nailed to the cross and speared in the chest during his crucifixion. He was supposed to have physically fought with the Devil and remarkably there was physical evidence in his monastery cell which gave credence to this. While these struggles were going on, unearthly sounds came from these battles after which Padre Pio bore horrible wounds which he could never have inflicted on himself.

I asked myself what was the best genre to write his story. What would reach the biggest audience? To write his biography as a history book would perhaps interest some catholic readers and a few readers who were into mysticism. That made for a rather limited market. But to write it as historical fiction created in my mind a much bigger market. After all, I thought this book could be written as a mild horror novel full of sex, violence and religion. That made for a much wider readership and if I stayed true to Padre Pio's biography and only fictionalized what went on with characters outside of the monastary, his story would reach far more readers that a pure history or biography. It made the project a lot more fun to write. My selection of genre was the correct one, since the book sold out 20,000 copies in hard cover. Now, since I own the rights, it has a good chance of being brought out again in paperback.

Will it serialize, can I make parts of it into articles?
Ask yourself if the original genre can also be turned out in another form. The Capuchin's story is certainly unique enough to be turned into several articles based on parts of his life. This has two great advantages; it makes for a new source of revenue*. It would help to promote the novel to a wider audience. Furthermore it would get Padre Pio's biography to many more readers, a primary motive for writing his story in the first place. Now there's an idea you can act on yourself. Buy my book, learn about Padre Pio and write your own stories about him. You may even think of another angle to pursue. You can't copyright a title or an idea so as long as you express the ideas in my book differently. It's fair game for anyone who wants to write it their way.

* For more ideas on how to get paid while promoting your book, please read Revenue Beyond Royalties by EJ Thornton **ISBN: 1-932344-39-X**

Define Your Niche

Where is your niche?

The most important thing is knowing where your niche is. Are you a poet, a novelist, a science-fiction writer, script writer or is your skill set in writing self-help books?

The best way to find out is by trying to write in several areas. When I first started writing seriously I began with a novel. Writing historical fiction was what I wanted to do most and I found it most fun. I was lucky and my first effort, ***"The Survivor of Babi Yar,"*** sold and was a success. My second effort was titled ***"The Capuchin,"*** also published and sold well. But then I found quite by accident that my real niche was to write self-help books. I found I had a skill in interpreting scientific, especially medical information, into lay language. It wasn't as much fun as writing novels, but I could turn them out a lot faster, they had a longer shelf life and self-help made a lot more money for me. Since then I've written about 10 to 1 self-help to novels.

What are your best writing skills?

Just as I discovered that self-help books were my real bread winners, you should put a great deal of thought into which markets will make you the greatest income. You have to eat. Don't let your first love stand in the way of making a good living. You may love writing poetry, and if so write all the poetry you want. But realize that poetry has a very limited market, and few poets can live on their poetry. However, if you have other writing skills, say writing advertising copy, newsletters, technical writing, non-fiction or children's stories that have a better earning potential, do what I've done, make your living writing what's in demand and write poetry for the love of it and sell what you can to supplement your income and fulfill your love.

Don't give up your day job, but also don't give up your love of writing what really satisfies your creative needs.

> *Make your living writing what's in demand!*

How can you make it the most interesting?

Once you've decided what your project is going to be, ask yourself how you can make it the most interesting final product possible. Say you decided to write a book about an event in the Civil War between the North and South in 1864. Do your writing skills dictate that you should write it as a straight history, or do you have the skills as a novelist to make it a far more interesting historical novel? The latter can put forth the same historical facts, but may have a far larger readership.

A great example of this is E. L. Doctorow's novel "The March,*" about General Sherman's march north toward Washington.

* The March by E.L. Doctorow **ISBN: 0812976150**

That's not to say that pure history can't be interesting if you have the talent to make it an exciting read. Abba Eban's book "My Country" illustrates this tactic well. There are many skilled historians that can make pure history read like a novel. Know your skills, your limitations and your passions.

How will you best reach your market?

Once you know your readers and you know your own skills and limitations, decide on your project by reexamining the best way to get your message out with the highest potential for success.

You have a subject for which you have a real passion to write. How can you best write it that will make it a magic read for your audience? One person who had an interest in the life of the Sioux Indians in the old West was John G. Neihardt. He wrote "Cycle of The West." He wrote the story of the Sioux Indians in several hundred pages of magnificent poetry. The story had already been well told in hundreds of pure history books, but this was his style. Were I to write a book about the Sioux Indians I'd not attempt it in either of those genre: I haven't the talent for either. I know my limitations and talents, so I'd need to select a portion of Sioux life that I feel some passion for; the atrocities of the Church Boarding Schools the Indian children were forced into to eliminate their language, values and religious beliefs and train them for lives of servitude. Since I'm no poet, nor am I enough of a scholar to write a pure history, I'd select to write it as an historic novel.

Know your readers, your market, your product and most important know thyself.

* My Country by Abba Eban **ISBN: 029799526X**

YOUR QUALIFICATIONS

What are your special qualifications to fill your niche?

If you are wondering if you are capable of writing a book because you've never been much of a speller, grammarian, or scholar, then my answer is yes, you are probably capable of writing a publishable book. Let me repeat, I've never made more than a C in any English, literature, or creative writing class that I ever took in grade school, high school or college. I'm still one of the worst spellers in the world, though I've improved that immensely just by having written so much over the years, which prove I'm somewhat trainable. If you're writing on a computer that wonderful machine will help you with grammar and spelling, and what it can't do an editor will probably fix. And if you can tell a good story, grammar and spelling will probably not be the things that will prevent publication.

If you can speak you can write.

So the next question then is, "Can you tell a good story in the written word? My answer to that is, "If you can speak you can write!" If you are capable of expressing yourself when you talk to people and make them understand what you're saying, you have the ability to do the same on paper in a manuscript.

> ## *Writing is probably the most forgiving of all art forms. . .*

There are great writers, there are good writers, there are mediocre writers and there are poor writers. And all have been published!

As an art form, writing is probably the most forgiving of all. That is because there are so many levels and types of readers that there is a market for almost any book. You're not the only person out there that likes your subject. There are readers out there that like what you have to say and will enjoy your way of saying it.

Know your limitations and your strong points.

At the risk of being repetitious, I have to reiterate that you know your limitations, your talents, your weaknesses and your strengths. Your weaknesses and limitations need not prevent you from writing a publishable book. If you know your frailties and are aware of them while you write, and especially when polishing your second and third drafts, you can over come these handicaps. That is also what editors are for. So, learn to write to your strong points!

Someone out there will like your style!

Always keep in mind that someone out there loves your writing, not just your mother. The happy news is that a lot more people out there will like your material, even if it's only for the information you can give them. More than likely, there are readers that will not only be interested in the substance of your book but also in your style.

TIME TO WRITE

Hurray! It's finally time to do what you want to do... start writing your book!

Equipment needed. Pencil, typewriter, computer... I know a writer of romance novels who writes with pencil on a yellow legal pad in her night gown and negligee, lying kitty-corner across her bed. I know another successful romance writer who had a special desk built that fits across her bath tub and writes on her lap top while soaking. Maybe these methods inspire them. Seems nuts to me, but use whatever works best for you.

When I first started writing, it was on an electric typewriter. That was a great improvement over the manual typewriter. Then the computer came along. What a difference: the computer will save you time and trouble. If you're one of the few people who are still computer resistant, take the plunge! If you're a paper and pencil or typewriter author, you'll have to rewrite or retype each draft you do, a horrible chore. Furthermore you won't have the benefit of, spell check, grammar check or the thesaurus. The best part is that you won't ever have to rewrite or retype drafts; all you'll have to do is read through the last draft you did and make your changes and corrections.

Other helpful aids and equipment are a good dictionary, thesaurus, encyclopedia, old magazines, other books on your topic, etc., etc., etc.

Hit libraries, bookstores and watch the news from time to time to keep current on your subject.

Throughout your writing, keep tabs on your competition and your market. Make sure you know the competition for your **PRODUCT!** Keep up with what changes may be going on in the world outside your writing area. A good place to keep tabs is on **www.Amazon.com, www.BarnesAndNoble.com, www.Google.com,** your nearest library, etc.

Keep an eye on changes in trends, attitudes and fads.

Keep an eye on changes in trends, attitudes and fads. They may influence your market and readers and their interests, attitudes and needs.

FIVE ELEMENTS

No matter what you are writing it is always a good idea to keep the five elements listed below in mind. In the news industry, every story should answer these six questions: What? Who? When? Where? How? Why?

Whatever you are writing you should answer the same questions, not necessarily in the same order. I've changed the names slightly to better fit our literary work.

Era or Time Period (When)

This is the period which the book spans. Immerse yourself in the period, its customs, lifestyle, habits, pastimes, etc. Flavor your book with nostalgia and social history. For fiction or non-fiction, this is equally important!

If your book is about World War II, as was my book "The Survivor of Babi Yar," it will probably span the early 1940's. Since the beginnings of WWII can be traced back to WWI, you may even deal with some events from the 1920's on, but the main emphasis would most likely be the late 1930's and early 1940's. That's the period you want to gain intimate knowledge of. Listen to the music of the time, what programs were on the radio, remember there was no TV. There were no jets and air travel for civilians was extremely rare. Trains were their main mode of transportation. There were no cruise ships, but ships were the major way to cross the seas. Meat was rationed. Gas was rationed. New tires were almost impossible to buy and car manufacturers stopped production of civilian vehicles. The more of these facts that you know the more real your book will seem. As your character walks down a street and sees people sitting on their front stoops because there was no air conditioning and he hears the Amos and Andy radio show coming from an open window, old timers will love the nostalgia and younger readers will find your story believable and will learn some things.

> *So how do you learn these life and social historical facts? Immersion!*

Read old newspapers of the time, old magazines, encyclopedias that were written in those times, listen to the music of the times, talk to old timers who lived in those times. Ask them questions. Prowl the libraries, museums and antique shops. The information is out there and if you want to write a great book of those times you have to learn the facts. They are out there and finding them can be lots of fun.

Place (Where)

Where do the events take place? Research the location and the location at that time period. Consider how to find the information. Non-fiction has to be accurate. Fiction has to be believable!

Immersion can help you here too. Read the magazines or the time, especially Life, Time, Look, Colliers, Newspapers, and especially National Geographic and the National Geographic Maps of the time. If you go to

Atlases make sure they are atlases of the time as the geography of the world has changed remarkably since WWI and WWII. Again old encyclopedias are a great source of geographic information … hit the antique stores. While you're at it, learn as much as you can about the politics of the time. Your characters would probably have been talking about the politics and the weather just like you do today. It will make things read real.

Story (Why)

This is what you want the reader to know after they've read the book. What would TV Guide write to describe your story? Give thought to your working title to keep you on track.

> *A book has a way of writing itself…*
> *Let it!*

But to keep yourself and your characters on track give yourself a working title and a sub title (a one sentence description of what you want it to say). The one sentence can be what you think you would write in TV guide to describe the story were it to be turned into a video show or if non-fiction a documentary.

I say "working title" because the publisher will have the last word about the title, a marketing decision. Sadly, sometimes your working title may be better than the publisher's creation. Some years ago I wrote a longevity self-help book with a working title "The Second Half Begins at Fifty." The publisher came up with the title "50 Plus." I still don't like it. I've rewritten the book and updated it, this publisher is sticking with **my** working title.

Give considerable thought to what you really want to tell your readers in your story. Don't be surprised if your book dictates some change while you write it. If it does, and it probably will change from your original concept some, consider what your book and your characters are telling you. Nothing is etched in stone until your publisher prints your first edition.

Plot (What & How)

Plots tell your reader how the story evolved. Plot is really several short stories which describe your characters, their actions, interrelations and where and how things happened.

Some writers plot a story all the way through before they begin to write. Some don't. I have a general idea of the story I want to tell. I have a general idea how I want to start, but then the book more or less writes itself. Most of the writers I've known write much the same way. If you can plot your book ahead then by all means do it. Always write the way that is easiest for you.

When I write a self-help book, I start with a table of contents which loosely outlines what I want in the book, but even that changes as I write and the book dictates new ideas as I progress with the work.

So all this raises the question, "How can I control what goes on in *my story?*"

The answer comes in the next and most important element of writing, characterization!

Characterization (Who)

This is by far the most important part of any book, fiction or non-fiction.

In non-fiction, case history of characters the reader can identify with or care about and what happened to them will keep them reading and make your points.

In fiction, characters the reader either loves or hates are what the reader will remember and will keep them reading. The only way to control your fiction is through your characters - who take on a life of their own. How to set limits on them so they do what you want is through careful profiling your characters. Do a very complete resume for each.

A street smart person will solve problems differently than a PhD in physics. Depending on the problems at hand the street smart may have an advantage over the PhD. If you know the background of your character, a background you assigned to him or her you will have some control as to how that character will respond to his environment and other characters. The more characteristics you assign to the characters in your story the more they will respond in the way you hope they will.

When I create a major character, I start with a birthday and year. I give them the education and profession or job I want for them. I determine what their parents are like and know a little about their siblings if they have any. This is information I may never use in the book, but it helps me know my characters. I put down a physical description, though I may not give a complete description in the book and leave a lot to the reader's imagination, but I don't want to forget and describe his or her blue eyes in chapter one and write about brown eyes in chapter eight. I want to have a good idea of the character's general personality and how he or she interacts with others. The more you know about your character, facts that you create, the more control you have in how that character will react in your story.

> *Your characters will do what they want but only within the characteristics you assign to them.*

I learned about how characters could take over from me in my first novel, ***"The Survivor of Babi Yar"*** when I created a very strong, bright woman resistance fighter. She started to take over from my main character, an 18 year old street wise kid. No matter how I tried to intervene, I couldn't get her to back off. She was just too smart and charismatic. To get her to take a back seat to my main character would have been contrived. I had no choice but to kill her off.

It is the characters who will keep your audience reading. They want to know what will happen to characters they love and hope to see the characters they dislike get their just rewards!

WRITERS BLOCK

Writer's block can be easily beat.

I learned to beat writer's block early on. I create a new character which begins a new plot and see how that character weaves into the story. It's like going to a sneak preview. If that doesn't work I may spend a few hours or days working on or starting another book. I frequently have more than one book in various stages just for that reason.

If nothing else works, I kill off someone in the story just to see what happens. You might just go to the internet and type in a keyword that deals with your writer's block problem and see what that leads to.

My publisher recommends* that if you're having problems writing your book that you write about your book. You're going to have to do this work anyway, so write the book synopsis by creating a promise to your readers - "What I want you to get out of this book is..." or write your bio by answering the question, "I am the only/perfect person to write this book because..." Taking a break from the book and looking at it from the outside can often get you past the momentary promise you're having.

* The Basics of Profitable Publishing by EJ Thornton **ISBN: 1-932344-50-0**

SET UP YOUR DOCUMENT TEMPLATE

There is a fairly standard format that most publishers like in the manuscripts they receive. It's a good idea to give them what they want.

❖ First, use white paper. *Colored paper will not get you favorable attention and it makes reading difficult.*

❖ Second, make sure you have ink in your printer so the black ink has good contrast with the white paper.

❖ Third, select a very readable font and make it no smaller than 12 point. The idea is to make the editor's read an easy one.

❖ Fourth, use double spacing throughout and print on only one side of the paper.

❖ Fifth, number each page in the upper right corner of the page.

❖ Sixth, in the upper left corner of each page put the title of your book below that, your full name as author. *Some writers add a phone numbers, but I've never found a need to do that.*

Once you've set up the format in your computer, it will take care of that on each page, a real blessing over typewriters.

These are good general guidelines to help you create your manuscript, but for more specific guidelines refer to each publisher's webpage or entry in the latest **Writer's Market.*** Follow those guidelines diligently.

---

* 2008 Writer's Market: **ISBN: 1582974969**

The First Draft

Start your first draft...

The most important advice I can give you in this book is, *"Puke it out as fast as you can!"* The keyword in this advice is *"Puke."* Why puke? Because until you get the first draft done you really don't know what the story will be like when finished. You want to see what your characters are going to do, what all your plots will turn out like and how close the story comes to what you started out to write. You'll know all this when the first draft is done and not much before. So puke it out, puke, puke, puke! Write almost as if you are in free association. That will let you write what's on your mind as well as what's on your character's minds.

1. Don't edit yet.

If you think you've written something that doesn't belong then save it someplace; don't pitch it. It may fit in later, give you an idea later or break a writer's block later. Something made you write it in the first place, it may work some place down the line. Create it all first, edit later.

> *You'll be as riveted to find out what happens to your characters as your readers will be.*

2. Let the book write itself. Don't harness its unique creative power.

Let me re-emphasize this point! If you recognize a typo as you make it, that's okay to correct, and if you're computer recognizes a grammatical error, okay - correct those as you go, but little else. For now, just write, write, write, write and write some more!

3. Get the story down and worry about polish later.

Polishing should wait until the second and third drafts. You may even want someone you trust do a read through to get their input before you start the second draft. Make sure they are interested in this type of book. For example, never critique someone's fantasy or science fiction book if you don't read them; you wouldn't have the foggiest idea if its a well written book for this genre.

> *Take what you like*
> *and leave the rest!*

Take the criticism with a grain of salt. You may be right in your creation of the part on paper, after all, this is your message, your calling, your passion - your book. Just give any feedback *you solicit* honest consideration before you act.

4. You don't know your book until you're done with draft one.

I have to repeat, you can't know what your book will turn out like until you've finished the first draft, so making major changes while doing your first draft may be folly.

5. Give it a rest before you start the second draft.

Give yourself at least a few weeks before starting your second draft. You want to get it out of your mind as much as possible, so that when you start the second draft it will be able to read it with a new approach.

I usually start another book. If I'm not in the mood to write something new or don't have a viable idea, I might take a vacation or get involved in a hobby or anything that takes my attention away from draft one.

Puke it out
as fast as you can!

DRAFT TWO

Tie up any loose ends.

As you read through your first draft, look for loose ends. If in chapter one a character leaves the room and says he's coming back later, make sure you bring him back later. If a murder weapon is dropped down a sewer don't forget about it. Make sure someone finds it and it doesn't just appear in the crime lab magically.

Flesh out the plot and the characters.

Remember how you puked out the first draft? Now is the time to clean up the mess. The second draft lets you flesh out the characters and the plots. Now that you know what the book is really about and how it got there, you should know your characters a lot better than when you started. Now you should flesh them out so your reader can get to know them better in the early part of your story.

The same goes for the plots and subplots that tell your story. Flesh them out so they are easily understood. Make sure they flow well from one to the next and that they make sense. Be wary of telling a story that is confusing to the reader. Remember that you have a visual picture of what you are writing. If you don't give your readers that same image, they have no way of knowing what you intended them to see. The second draft is where you should read through critically and make necessary changes to resolve your concerns.

When I wrote my second novel **"The Capuchin,"** during the second draft editing, I put the third chapter first. I decided that the book made more sense that way. After shuffling things about a bit, it turned into a much better book.

Polish, polish, polish … and polish some more….

The second draft is where you should correct your typos, spelling boo-boos, and infractions of grammar rules.*

If grammar rules are abused in dialogue that may be okay. After all, none of us speak alike and some of us slaughter the language. That may add character to your characters.

While you polish look for redundancies; some things you may want to repeat for effect or to remind the reader of an important point long past, but too much of repetition can get boring and insult the reader's intelligence..

The first draft
is an 110,000 word outline
for a 100,000 word book!

---

*Elements of Style by Strunk & White **ISBN: 0143112724**

ALL SUBSEQUENT DRAFTS

Third draft, fourth draft, etc., etc., etc...

If you know someone you trust to give you good constructive feedback let them read it, **but** be sure they like your type of book. Take their comments seriously, espeically if you solicited their comments, but also take it with a grain of salt. They could be wrong.

If they find errors you missed in the second draft, great! But ask them to be on the lookout for any parts of your story or plots that are confusing or unclear. See if they think there are any dangling storylines in the book. You may have left out details that you saw in your mind's eye but neglected expressing well enough to your reader.

If you can't find a friend to read through the manuscript, put it away for a few weeks after the second draft and then give it another critical read yourself. Keep in mind that it is very hard to proof read your own work because more than likely you'll make the same mistakes over and over again.

Now the sub-title of this chapter is "Third draft, fourth draft, etc., etc., etc." Don't take that too seriously, please. I've known too many writers who were obsessive about their work. It was never quite good enough so they re-wrote and rewrote and rewrote again and again and again. The one thing they never did do was finish their manuscript. After having written well over twenty published books, rarely do I do more than two drafts. That's not because I'm such a fantastic writer now, (though I've improved considerably since my first attempts almost thirty years ago), but because I've learned that if I've done my research, have a good project and I like what I've written, by the end of the second draft there is probably a publisher out there who will also like it. If the idea is a good one, and I've shown the publisher that his readers are going to be the right market for this project, he'll let me know what changes I may have to make to improve the book for their readers.

Force yourself to contact a publisher at least by the end of the third draft. I'll tell you how in the next chapter!

GETTING A PUBLISHER

Research the book stores and libraries for your kind of publisher.

Yes, it's time to market research again, but this time it will only take you a day or two.

Head for your local library and then go to the biggest book store in your town. Go to the section in both where your type of book is shelved; be it mystery, history, romance, self-help, whatever. Now pick over the books there and see which ones are most like yours: consider length, story lines, reading level, even styles of writing. Look especially at books that you think you would like to read.

Having done that list all the publishers that published those books you've selected. There will probably be at least five or more, maybe as many as a dozen. Those are the most likely publishers to buy your book! Most publishers have fairly well defined readers. They know those readers intimately, know what they want. That's why publishers that put out pure history may not be interested in mystery, romance or self-help. Scientific publications are usually published by publishers who know the science well and know scientific readers well. A few very big publishers will do a very broad book list, but even they have limits and may even have a different imprint for different genre.

So now that you've zeroed in on your potential publishers, **what next?**

> ## Don't write...
> ## Call!!!

Don't write ... CALL!

I've had over twenty books published with numerous publishers and I've never written a single query letter. Query letters are dangerous; I think they are harder to write than the book was. You may have a great book, but if your query letter isn't great, your book will never be seen by a publisher. I have all the confidence in the world when I write a book or article, but if I'd have to write a one page letter to sell that book, I'd be anxious because it might not get the book's qualities or points across. You can take courses on how to write the "perfect" query letter, but unless you know the editor you're writing to, you can't know what he or she considers a perfect query letter.

So what do I think you should do?

Talk to the editors!

You've found your potential publishers in the library and book stores. Now return to the library and look into the latest *Writer's Markets*. If you'd rather, you can buy your own copy, but most if not all libraries have them for your free use. You probably won't be able to check out the current printing, but you only need it long enough to look up the publishers you've selected.

When you find your various publishers' listings you'll find their addresses, phone numbers, fax numbers, e-addresses and possibly a website. More important you'll get a description of the type books they want. Check that against your own research. Even more important than that is the listings of all their editors, their specialty if they have one, like non-fiction, fiction, mystery, health, etc., etc., etc. If no specialty is listed, which will be the case in most listings, pick the name that you think you'd like to speak with most. This is strictly a comfort decision.

Now call. He or she will more than likely talk to you. Realize that editors make their money by buying good books, not turning down phone calls. If the first one you call is out or refuses your call, try another on the editor list. One of them is sure to accept your call. Once you reach the editor say something like, "Ms. Jackson, my name is…" introducing yourself. "I've written a manuscript which is typical of the books you publish." And then succinctly describe your story. If you did your research well, you should impress the editor by emphasizing the points of similarity in your story and their reader's interests. Then add, "May I send you a copy via e-mail attachment?" I've found that in all most all calls I've ever made, the answer is "yes." If it happens to be a "no," you've lost nothing, just call the next editor on your list… **Even one who works for the same publishing house.**

I've found this method easiest and most comfortable for me, and quite successful. Do what is most comfortable for you. By not sending a query letter I've bypassed what is called "over the transom solicitation," sending a letter or manuscript unsolicited to compete with the hundreds of other unsolicited inquiries publishers receive weekly.

When you get your positive reply, e-mail your attached manuscript with a very short note to remind the editor of you phone call. Don't put it off until he or she can forget about your phone conversation.

Most publishers prefer to receive manuscripts electronically. It's less paper to have to handle, when they purchase your book it is easier for them to check and edit, and when it's time to print it doesn't have to be typeset.

Editors make their living buying good books, not turning down phone calls!

SELF PUBLISHING HAS CHANGED

I have a new attitude toward self publishing!

The publishing industry has changed dramatically in the past decade. The internet has made an unbelievable change in how books can be published. It's not just that you don't have to go to the expense of copying your manuscript for every publisher you send to, but self publishing has really come into its own.

Ten years ago, I would have advised you to steer completely clear of self-publishing, unless you were a lecturer and could sell your book at the 'back of the room.' In those days self publishing was also called "Vanity publishing." You paid you money, anywhere from a few to $10,000 and a few weeks or months later you got a delivery of 500 to a thousand or more books delivered to your door. Then you'd find that book stores would rarely if ever take your books. Unless you had a lot of friends to give birthday, anniversary and Christmas gifts to, you'd have a hell of a storage problem for several years. That has all changed. There are still a few Vanity publishers out there and a few crooks that will scam you, but if you do your due diligence on the many self or "Partner publishers,*" you should find a safe, affordable solution for publication of your book.

*Getting-Published.com

Partner Publishing: a new twist to the old way of Self Publishing!

My first 20 books were published by contract with conventional publishing houses; this book and six others I'm contracted with a "Partnership Publisher."

Why? I'll tell you why!

1. Money! Where with a conventional publisher you'll get between 10% and 15% of the gross price of you book and sometimes less, with the Partner Publisher you'll get almost all the profit over the actual cost of publishing the book. It your book sells for $15.00 you may get $8 to $10 for each book sold, depending on how big your press run is, instead of $1.50 to $ 2.50 or less per book:

2. If you would go a conventional publisher and got a contract today, it could take up to eighteen months to hit the book stores. Partner publishing has taken less than three months for each of these books!

3. With the internet, websites, e-mail, Amazon, Barnes and Noble and innumerable links to related sites, your book has the potential of reaching hundreds of potential readers 24 hours a day 7 days a week 52 weeks a year.

4. It is no longer necessary to warehouse your books; in most cases the partner publisher takes care of that. Furthermore with modern day electronics books can be run in numbers of 250 or less and reorders can be delivered in days or a few weeks.

5. Most partner publishers have established marketing programs and also help you to develop your own sales channels to help you increase sales.

The world of book publishing and sales has changed drastically with the advent of the internet!

It's no longer a matter of book stores not buying your books, the number of books sold via computer today may well surpass what is sold in brick and mortar stores. Almost all the books I've purchased in the past two years have been purchased off the internet. It's easier, often cheaper and more fun to browse.

We'll review the differences between Commercial Publishing, Self Publishing and Partner Publishing again and their differences in a later chapter regarding publisher's contracts.

GETTING AN AGENT

After you get a publisher it's a lot easier.

Over the years, I've had three different agents. The first was William Morris, a huge agency out of New York. My agent within the agency was Pam Bernstein, a very congenial agent who did her best for me, but she also had such authors as Henry Kissinger and I wasn't at the head of her priority list. I soon discovered it was not best to be a little fish in a big pond.

The second agent was a local agency in Denver where I live. My thought was that face to face would make for a better relationship. It did make for great rapport, but even after a year's relationship he still hadn't made a single sale. In the end I made a sale and used him to negotiate my contract. Shortly thereafter he retired.

The third agent was in California, Agent's Incorporated. They were quite aggressive and not only sold some books for me but also got for me a four book consignment from Prima Publishing with $125,000.00 in advances. Agents are worth their weight in gold!

The problem is that for a first time author, it is harder to get an agent than it is to find a publisher. So, this being the case, how can you get a good agent? Well there is the query letter, which will probably have no better results in getting an agent than in getting a publisher. I've always found the best way to get an agent is to get a publisher first and then contact an agent to negotiate a contract. So why involve an agent when you've already done his or her job of getting a publisher? Why have to pay the agent 10% to 15% of my royalties if I've made the sale of my book? Because an agent can negotiate a better contract than I ever could. Another thing I've learned, I never used an attorney to deal with a publisher. They don't understand the publishing industry and I've seen where an attorney actually lost a publisher for an author.

I've found that once you've gotten a publisher interested, agents will take you far more seriously and will be far less likely to say "No" to you.

Of course if you enter into Partner or Self Publishing an agent becomes unnecessary, unless you need someone to negotiate publishing rights to another publisher, movie or TV producer or for foreign rights. More about that when we talk about contracts in the next chapter...

Publishing Contracts

What to watch out for...
What to demand!

There are four major publishing options. They are Commercial Publishing, Vanity Publishing, Self Publishing and the newest kid on the block, Partner Publishing. Each has its own unique policies and advantages or disadvantages. Let's check these differences out by examining differences in their different contracted specifications as compared to the commercial publishing houses.

The Commercial Publisher

The advance

Commercial publishing is what most of us think of when we start to think about seeing your book in print. We dream of this fantastic advance and a fortune in royalties. Up until a few years ago this was what most authors would strive for - a book contract from a famous publishing house.

When you get signed by a commercial publisher you may or may not get an advance. If there is an advance it is rarely larger than your royalties would be on the first printing of usually no more than 3,000 to 5,000 books. If your book was priced at $20.00 and you had a first time royalty of 10% of gross, you might get an advance of

$6,000 to $10,000. That is an advance against sales, so before you get any further royalties that first printing has to sell out. Then it's up to the publisher if any further printings occur. Most first time authors never see a second printing.

In the case of the Vanity Publisher, there is no advance except for the advance *you pay* to them to print and deliver your book to your door, for storage and distribution. The Vanity Publisher has no further obligation to you. Cost to you could be anywhere from a $2,000 to $10,000 to the most typical $20,000 or more, depending on the cost of printing, binding, design, size of the printing run and shipping charges, among other charges.

As for Self Publishing, it's all up to you. You arrange the design of the book, the cover art, the type setting or digital type and printing. You deal with the bindery and then take delivery of all the books. Cost is up to how well you can negotiate with your suppliers, artists, printers, binders, shippers, etc. It will be an interesting experience and quite worth the learning curve if you ever plan on doing this again! It will probably be less costly to you than the Vanity Publishers. Once books are delivered, you will be on your own to distribute and sell your product.

Partner Publishing also will pay you no advance. But all production work is done by the publisher. You'll pay for the production costs but probably far less than with either Vanity or Self publishing. The big difference is you won't have to take delivery on a ton of books and you'll have established marketing and sales channels.

Publication Rights

Publication rights are what you are selling to the Commercial Publisher. That means they own everything about your book except the copyrights, which you should never sell or relinquish. If you give up your copyrights you can never use any part of what you have written without written permission of the copyright holder. Very few, if any Commercial Publishers will demand the copyrights to your book. What they are buying from you is the right to produce, market and sell your book. They also have the right to resell your book to another publisher, for domestic or foreign publication, to movie or TV production or any other use of your product. That's not a bad thing because your contract should state that you get 50% of whatever they get for the resales.

With Vanity, Self and Partner publishing you keep all your rights in most cases.

Never sell your copy rights!

Length of contract

Length of contract with most Commercial Publishers varies, but in most cases is for a year or two, however they usually put in a clause for First Right of Refusal, which means that any book you write during the length of the contract you **have to offer** to them first. That's not a bad thing!

With Vanity Publishers the contract is usually for a single printing so there are no term limits.

If you Self-Publish, you may have contracts with all your vendors and suppliers, and those will only be for an individual job basis.

In the case of Partnership Publishing, you will have a partnership contract for each book you do with them, but you'll determine the length of the contract. You can get out of it at any time you may want to make other arrangements for further publications or printings. Furthermore, you are free to negotiate with any other publisher at any time.

Author's warranties

In Commercial Publishing, the publisher owns all rights to your book until they decide to terminate the contract. You will hopefully retain the copyrights, but any time you want to use any part of your work during the contract you will have to get their permission.

Vanity Publishing is a mixed bag. In some cases they claim all rights and copyrights. It is up to you to negotiate a contract that protects you. Read all the small print!!!

With Self Publishing and Partner Publishing, you - the author own all rights and copyright. But with the Partner Publisher, you give them permission to print.

Book price and discounts

In Commercial Publishing, the publisher sets all prices and discounts. Retail price of the book will depend on cost of production and what the market will bear. If the book does not sell, the publisher has the right to "remainder" the book often at pennies on the dollar and you will not get any royalty from remaindering as the publisher usually sells at a loss.

> *If at all possible,*
> *buy your own remaindered books*
> *and sell them yourself!*

With Vanity Publishing, the printer sets the wholesale price and you determine retail and any discounts your may want in marketing.

As a Self Publisher, your wholesale price is the total cost of production and shipping. You will set the retail price and any marketing deductions you feel necessary. Factor in your pre-press costs with the size of your print run - make sure you'll see a return on your up front investment.

As a Partner Publisher, your partner will set the wholesale price of the book and you will set retail and any discounts.

Royalties

In Commercial Publishing, the royalty is usually 10% to 15% of the retail price of the book. In some cases, you might be able to get a sliding scale starting usually at 10% and increasing with future printings, should there be any.

With Vanity Publishing, your royalty is the difference between your costs of production and whatever you can sell the book for. If your production expenses are not too high and retail is priced right you might get 50% more of retail to keep. Remember, if you sell your book to retail stores typically take 60% of retail, leaving you very little profit if any. Vanity books are best sold at lectures and events you may take part in. Many end up as gifts or in storage.

As Self Publisher, wholesale is your production costs, you set all retail and discount prices. Marketing problems are similar to Vanity Publishing.

As a Partner Publisher your partner will set the wholesale price that the book can be sold to retail establishments or wholesalers. Your profit is the difference between the wholesale and retail price of the book, often up to 70% of your retail sales.

Distribution

Commercial Publishers will distribute your book through their established channels. Order fulfillment will not be your problem nor will you have to deal with returns.

You will have all the responsibility of sales and distribution of Vanity Publications. It is *very rare* for Vanity Publications to be carried by retail book stores or wholesalers.

As a Self Publisher you will have the same distribution problems as the Vanity author ... all sales and distribution problems are yours.

As a Partner to the Partner Publisher your books will be distributed through the publisher's already established channels. Those order fulfillments will not by your problem, nor should warehousing of the books. If in addition, you can set up your own distribution and as a lecturer, via Web sites, e-mail or other methods. You are free to do so and even encouraged and if necessary, taught how. This activities will markedly raise your income.

These are some of the major differences in the various publishing options you have. Chose whichever you feel most comfortable with. I personally would only consider Commercial Publishing or Partner Publishing.

MARKETING

Marketing yourself, marketing your books

Well, your book is finally a reality! Regardless of how you decided to have it published, it's a long dreamed of reality. Congratulations on a job well done!

> ## *Throw yourself a "Launch Party!"*

Have a party to celebrate the event with friends, relations, colleagues and other acquaintances. Have numbered and autographed copies available for them to buy. Even provide a quantity discount to encourage multiple sales. You'll be amazed at how many people will buy a copy for one of their friends too, usually just to brag that they 'know the author.'

However you have other jobs to do while celebrating this completion...

Even though your publisher, if you selected a commercial or partner publisher, will do what they can to promote and market your book, the more you do to market yourself and your book, the greater its sales will be. **Very few books ever become best sellers without tremendous effort on the parts of publisher and** *author!*

Since you're a writer, a professional writer and author, write. Now that you've written a book it's time to write about the book and about yourself. Your publisher may have a publicist working on this too, but you are by far the most passionate about the book, know it best and thus can be a tremendous help in its promotion. Your publisher will be most interested in promoting your book to retailers and wholesalers to get it introduced into their marketing channels. Your job is to get the readers excited so the wholesalers and retailers will get orders and reorders. Your job is to get publicity, *not advertising.*

The Press Kit

The first thing you should do is prepare a press kit. Your publisher may do this in which case your help will be appreciated. After all, who knows better than you why you wrote the book and why you are the best person to have written it.

The Press Kit should be brief, to the point, and be comprised of three main parts: the press release, a biography of you the author and a list of interview questions.

The press release has to grab the interest of your intended target, a news editor, radio producer, TV producer or anyone who can get you an audience to hear about you and your book.

It should be no longer than one page as it is in competition with many press releases that attack these people daily. ***It needs a headline that grabs their attention and piques their interest immediately.*** Then the release should tell what the book will do for the reader, what it will teach, how it will make the reader happier, wealthier, calmer, healthier or whatever.

The second part of the Press Kit is your Biography. It too must be brief and to the point, again no longer than a page. It should tell why you are the best person to have written this book, what your credentials for writing it are. If you have some human interest facts about yourself that relate directly to the topic of, or reason for writing the book, add it briefly.

The third part of the Press Kit is a list of interview questions. Since the major point of the press kit is to get interviews in the various medias, you can make the work of the interviewer easier by giving him an interesting page of questions. It is also nice to have questions asked that you can field well.

As a sample, I'll share with you the press release I wrote for my books, "Heavy and Healthy ... Forget your weight and get fit." and "Sex in the Golden years ... the best Sex ever." Notice that the titles go a long way to tell you what the books are about.

It needs to fit on one full size page of paper and should be double spaced in a font size 12 or greater. This reprint does not follow complete correct formatting.

September 25th 2007
FOR IMMEDIATE RELEASE

Thornton Publishing
17011 Lincoln Ave. #408
Parker, Colorado 80134
Fax: 720-863-2013
Phone: 303-794-8888
Contact EJ Thornton
publisher@BooksToBelieveIn.com

Heavy and Healthy ... Forget Your Weight and Get Fit by **Othniel J. Seiden, MD & Jane L. Bilett, PhD** −Clinical Psychologist

Medicine today places far too much emphasis on America's weight, often ignoring much more important indications of your actual health status. This book is written for St. Bernards who for years have been trying every diet around, hoping to become Greyhounds ... and have finally realized that **St. Bernards can't change into Greyhounds**. We are a sizable (no pun intended) group, for **only five percent of all dieters ever keep off what they take off.** So what's the next best hope? Well if we have to remain St. Bernards, let's become the healthiest St. Bernards we can possibly be. And in addition, **let's learn to be happy as St. Bernards.**

If you've been yo-yoing your weight up and down for the past decade or two it's time to try a new approach. **Folks who are destined to be heavy can indeed be healthy.** Weight is only one factor in our total health profile, and if you can get the other factors in line, **your weight need make little difference;** in fact it will probably correct itself.

The word Diet does not appear in this book! Diets rarely work. You may knock off 20, 25, 30 pounds ... but as soon as you go off a diet, you'll gain back 25, 35, 45 pounds or more weight than you originally lost. Sound familiar? Remember, national averages show that less than five percent of all of us ever keep off the weight from all the diets we've tried.

If you follow this program you'll never diet again! And, if you follow this program, **a year from today you'll in the best shape you can be ... possibly the best you have ever been ... in spite of your weight!** That's the goal and the guarantee of this book pure and simple.

Bio

Jane Bilett, PhD has practiced Clinical Psychology for over 30 years, **Othniel J. Seiden, MD,** has been a physician well over 40 years. Together they're well qualified to help you become the healthiest person you can be, mentally and physically, in spite of your weight.

In over 40 years of practicing medicine virtually all over the world, in both modern industrial countries and in the Third World, at both general medicine and emergency medicine, Dr. Seiden recognized that a great number of heavy people were in the best of health and as frequently skinny folks were frequently in the worst of health. Weight was usually not the determining factor. Healthy people, in spite of their weight, have certain other indications of their physical condition and longer life, while the unhealthy patients lack many of these true health indicators. Heavy people with these good physical indicators were healthy and enjoyed more longevity while slim people without these other more important measures were sickly and usually had shorter life expectancy. To bring these favorable health factors in line with good health and longevity actually require rather simple and few life style changes.

Dr. Jane Bilett in her 30 plus years of clinical practice has seen the distress, anxiety, depression and lack of self esteem that a warped self image of too many of those people designated as over weight or obese suffer. She has helped hundreds of these patients to improve their self image, confidence and self esteem. Her most important contribution to this book is to show how heavy people can learn to see their true self worth and to make the few and simple life style changes necessary to succeed in turning their heath status around. This, their book and program will show you how you can be both Heavy and Healthy! With this book and your doctor you can become the healthiest you've ever been!

Interview Questions

With all the talk today about the dangers of obesity and overweight, how can you claim that a person can be heavy and healthy?

What should the reader of Heavy and Healthy expect to learn?

Surely you're not suggesting that it is better to be overweight or obese than slim?

I've read and heard a great deal about BMI or Body Mass Index over the past years to be the best index of weight and health. How do you reconcile this with your book? (Answer about 45 seconds)

What about the fact that America is having an explosion, almost an epidemic of Diabetes due to overweight and obesity?

What are the other indexes or measures that we should concentrate on getting in line rather than weight to achieve good health and longevity?

What longevity are we to aim for?

You talk about a few simple life style changes that will turn your health status around, what are they?

How can people who are overweight gain the confidence, improved self image and feelings of self-worth you write about in the book Heavy and Healthy?

I see that this book is part of a series your publisher calls The Boomer Book Series; what other books have you written for this series?

Do you have other titles planed for the future of this series?

I assume form the name of this series it is aimed at the Baby Boomers, people over the age of 50 or 60. Isn't that rather late in life to start making life style changes to improve your health?

I'm amused by the title of your book "Sex In The Golden Years … the best sex you've ever had!" Isn't that a time when sex slows down considerably?

Your books seem to be going against the trend in what most of us and many doctors think about the Baby Boomer years. What makes you such a renegade?

Well, I'd say your books give us youngsters something to look forward to!

September 25th 2007
FOR IMMEDIATE RELEASE

Thornton Publishing
17011 Lincoln Ave. #408
Parker, Colorado 80134
Fax: 720-863-2013
Phone: 303-794-8888
Contact EJ Thornton
publisher@BooksToBelieveIn.com

Sex In The Golden Years, The Best Sex You've Ever Had! By Othniel J Seiden, MD and Jane L. Bilett, PhD

It's been argued that sex is mainly intended for procreation, but in our "Golden Years" sex has two main and important purposes, to give us extreme pleasure and strengthen our relationship. While many people consider themselves over the hill sexually after 45 or 50 or menopause, with a little change in attitudes and techniques almost all of us can achieve the best sex for ourselves and our partners that we've ever had at any age. Today research with the elderly shows quite clearly that the human animal is designed to be sexually active throughout life. Couples in their 60s, 70s, 80s and older frequently consider their sex life as important as ever and happily more fun and pleasurable than ever.

The purpose of this book is to dispel myths about "senior sex" and provide the skills and attitudinal changes that can keep us sexually eager and active literally forever. It will give us the knowledge and skills to give our partner the greatest pleasure and satisfaction ever experienced. Both men and women can learn to easily achieve multiple orgasms and sustain their lovemaking until both are completely satisfied.

In majority of cases where couples are not completely satisfied in the quality or quantity of their sexual relationships the causes can be identified and remedied by reading this book, only a few might require further therapy or coaching. Sex In The Golden Years will help you to rekindle your romance and ignite your love life to an intensity never before achieved. After all, *if the good Lord didn't want you to do it, He wouldn't have made it feel so good!*

If necessary answers can be given in less time to fit program needs.

Bio

Jane Bilett, PhD has practiced Clinical Psychology for over 30 years, **Othniel J. Seiden, MD,** has been a physician well over 40 years. Together they're well qualified to help you achieve the best sex you've ever had at any age.

In over 40 years of practicing medicine virtually all over the world, in both modern industrial countries and in the Third World, at both general medicine and emergency medicine, Dr. Seiden recognized that a great number of elderly people stated that they enjoyed the best personal and sexual relationship with their partners than at any other time in their lives. Furthermore, those who were dissatisfied with their sex life, the problems were easily identified and in most cases remedied with minimum changes or simple tweaking of attitudes or techniques.

Dr. Jane Bilett in her 30 plus years of clinical practice has seen the distress, anxiety, depression and lack of self esteem or warped self image of too many of those patients suffered who interpreted their diminished relationship with partners and lack luster sex lives. She has helped hundreds of these patients to improve their relationship and sex lives at the same time improving self image, confidence and self esteem.

Combining their experiences, Seiden and Bilett joined to write *Sex In The Golden Years ... The best sex ever* to help the Baby Boom generation to recharge their sex lives and strengthen their relationship to levels beyond their wildest dreams. Wow!

NOTICE: They are not the same bio. Each bio is different

for each book!

> *You'll be surprised how many book stores will be happy to have you in for a signing. Just ask!*

Interview Questions

I'm amused by the title of your book "Sex In The Golden Years ... the best sex you've ever had!" Isn't that a time when sex slows down considerably?

Most of us think of people in their senior years slowing down in all areas of their lives, how can you claim that a person's sex life can be better than any time in their lives?

What should the reader of _Sex In The Golden Years_ expect to learn?

Why have we always been led to believe that as we aged past 40, 50 or older or women after menopause that sex tapered off and took a back seat to other things in our lives?

With all the adds we see on TV about ED or erectile dysfunctions, how do you reconcile this with your book?

You mention that both men and women can easily learn to have multiple orgasms and that premature ejaculation is one of the easiest sexual dysfunctions to remedy. How is this accomplished?

You talk about a few simple changes that will turn your sex life around, what are they?

How can people gain the confidence, improved self image and feelings of self-worth you write about in the book _Sex In The Golden Years_?

I see that this book is part of a series your publisher calls The Boomer Book Series; I what other books have you written for this series?

Do you have other titles planed for the future of this series?

I assume from the name of this series it is aimed at the Baby Boomers, people over the age of 50 or 60. Isn't that rather late in life to start making changes to improve your sex life and strengthen your relationship?

Your books seem to be going against the trend in what most of us and many doctors think about the Baby Boomer years. What makes you such a renegade?

Well, I'd say your books give us youngsters something to look forward to!

If you'd like and it can all fit on the page, you can tell the interviewer how long you expect your answer to be. Practice these questions with someone who will give you constructive feedback. The more you can speak freely - instead of read a given answer off a sheet - the better interviewee you'll be. The host will cut out questions if necessary to fit their program needs.

There are Marketing Firms and Publicists, who can do promotion of you and your book, and your publisher may take care of all this, but they usually do not spend much to promote a first time author. Before you spend your own money on a publicist or marketing firm try to do it yourself. Feel free to write your bio in third person as if someone else is bragging about you.

BOOK SIGNINGS

Your publisher may offer local stores in your home area book signings. By all means, let them know you are more than willing to participate. It is the best way to get your name out in your home town, get local publicity and news interviews and sell books.

If your publisher doesn't help you with this type promotion, you'll be surprised how many book stores will be happy to have you in for a signing. Just ask! Don't count on the publisher or the publicist to know your local area - you know it best. Take the reigns and do it yourself. The experience is very valuable!

When you do set up a signing, let your publisher know so there will be adequate books for the audience to buy.

Readers really are bedazzled by authors.

Be prepared to speak about your book and answer questions your audience will have. The more you interact with them, the more books you'll sell. If you do a good job with the staff, they'll likely recommend your book to their customers!

INTERNET BOOK SALES

Books are the most sold item on the internet.

However just having your book on the internet does not guarantee its sales. Even though there may be more book sales on the internet than in book stores now, for best results you have to put forth some effort. Certainly, the internet has changed the book industry dramatically and it has given the beginning author an advantage they didn't have 20 some years ago.

Step one is getting a website.

Step two is getting traffic to your website!

Step three is getting them to buy from your website!

> *Once you've written a book,*
> *you are an authority on the subject!*

As wonderful a place to sell books as the internet is, you have to compete with **literally millions** of other authors. You have to find a way to attract readers to you site over those of the competition. You should get a web domain for both your book and for your name. To attract readers to your Web pages you might consider E-mail campaigns, link exchanges, Web rings, classified ads, bid rank search engines and content based pages. When you send out an e-mail notifying all your friends and even enemies, every time your Web site is hit it is tracked by the search engine. The tracker does not know or care who the hit is from. It only counts how many hits there are from how many computers. The more hits, the higher you go up on whatever indexes you get onto like Amazon.com or BarnesandNoble.com.

Nothing has influenced and changed the book and publishing business more than the internet. Take advantage of it. Learn as much about how the internet works as you can. Look at other websites of authors, of successful book sellers, of best-selling authors.

Learn how to adapt the ideas you like to your own

Websites are marketing tools. They're also popularity contests, so develop as many links to your webpages as you possibly can.

Books are the highest selling items on the internet and every year a larger percentage of books are sold on the internet than in brick and mortar book stores. **Get your fair share of the business.**

Radio and TV

Local and sometimes even national radio and TV interviews are sometimes remarkably easy to get. Your Press Kit will go a long way to getting these interviews. If your publisher doesn't get you a list of radio and TV shows that interview writers or arrange interviews for you try the local yellow pages and send a kit to your local media on your own. If your interview is good and gets local attention it won't be long before other media will bid for your attention.

There are over 900 talk shows out there begging for material to broadcast to their listeners. Let them know what you've got.

* http://SabahRadioShows.com - For more information on how to get on the radio.

SPEAKING ENGAGEMENTS

Get your fair share of the 'back of the room!'

Service clubs like Rotary, Kiwanis, church groups, ladies groups, synagogues, schools, all are fair game for speaking engagements and are usually looking for speakers for their gatherings. Let them know about you and your book. Usually they will let you sell your product at the end of your talk.

If your book is really unique and has broad interest consider getting on a lecture tour. Nothing sells books faster than seminars and if your book deals with business or industry a lecture tour speaking at business seminars can turn into a gold mine for you. Once you've written a book you are an authority on your subject and others want to hear what you have to say. Give it to them!

There are Writer's Clubs all over the U.S. When you're a published writer you have information they want. Give it to them!

There are writer's conferences* all over the country. When you are a published author you have information they want. Give it to them!

There are business clubs all over the U.S. When you are a published writer and your book is in any way business related, you have information they want. Give it to them!

* For a listing of the major writing conferences around the country, use Shaw Guides: http://Writing.ShawGuides.com

RESOURCES & RECOMMENDED READING

Profitable Book Publishing by EJ Thornton
ISBN: 1932344500
Revenue Beyond Royalties by EJ Thornton
ISBN: 193234439X
Accelerated Book Marketing by EJ Thornton
ISBN: 193234439X
Elements of Style by William Strunk & E.B.White
ISBN: 0143112724

Chicago Manual of Style: **ISBN: 0226104036**

2011 Writer's Market: **ISBN: 1582979480**

The March by E.L. Doctorow **ISBN: 0812976150**

My Country by Abba Eban **ISBN: 029799526X**

Secrets to Creating Passive Income **ISBN: 0980194199**

Empowered Self-Publishing getting-published.com
Shaw Guides WritingShawGuides.com
Getting on the Radio SabahRadioShows.com

BoomerBookSeries.com

Consulting About Your Book

Otti Seiden (the author) and/or EJ Thornton (the publisher) are available for consultation about your book project on an hourly basis.

To contact them about your book and to schedule an appointment or to see a list of services provided, please

Email

Query@BooksToBelieveIn.com

More From Othniel

Health

5 HTP The Serotonin Connection:
The Natural Supplement that helps
you be in control of your mind and body!
ISBN: 1519148445
5-HTP and Depression Management:
Available in Kindle Only
5HTP and Memory Loss Management with:
Available in Kindle Only
5 HTP PMS and Menopause:
Available in Kindle Only
Coping with Arthritis:
ISBN: 151941353X
Coping with BPH:
Benign Prostatic Hypertrophy
Male, over 45, you probably have it!
Available in Kindle Only
Coping with Colorectal Cancer:
Prevention and Cure of theSecond Leading
Cause of Cancer Deaths
Available in Kindle Only
Coping with Fibromyalgia:
It's not in your head, it's a disease!
ISBN: 1519438311

Coping with Prostate Cancer:
Prevention and Cure
of Man's Most Common Cancer
ISBN: 1519438737

Heart of a Woman:
Prevetion and Cure of the #1 Killer in Women
ISBN: 1519441533

Heavy and Healthy:
Forget Your Weight and Get Fit!
ISBN: 1519495412

Quit Smoking Now!:
The Program to Help You
Quit Smoking Now and Forever!
ISBN: 1519495781

Sharpening the Aging Mind:
Methods, Tricks & Tips to
Keep Your Mind Super Sharp
ISBN: 1519496028

Sleep Disorders Management:
Available in Kindle Only

The Second half begins at 50:
Your Longevity Handbook
ISBN: 1519496389

Walk!:
Walk Your Way to Great Health & Long Life
Available in Kindle Only

Weight & Appetite Management:
Available in Kindle Only

Relationships:

Adultery Case Histories:
Why People Cheat on Their Partners
Available in Kindle Only

Communing with the Dead:
Death Needn't Part You
ISBN: 1519190085

Foreplay:
The True Focus of Great Sex
ISBN: 1519440979

Sex in the Golden Years:
The Best Sex Ever, Stay Sexually Active for Life
ISBN: 1519495927

The Big O:
Male & Female Multiple Orgasms
ISBN: 1519496109

The Hospice Experience:
Making Your Most Important Final Decision
ISBN: 1519496281

When Your Spouse Dies:
A widow's & widower's handbook
ISBN: 151949646X

Jewish Fiction

Padre Pio:
The Capuchin – the life of Padre Pio -
St. Pio of Pietrelcina
Sex, Horror & Violence vs. Unyielding Faith!
ISBN: 1519495684

Seed of Avraham:
A 4000 Year History of the Jewish Family...
ISBN: 1519495811

Shtetl:
The Story of a Life No More...
As told from the hereafter
ISBN: 1519496036

The Cartographer:
1492
ISBN: 151949615X

The Condemned Voyage:
The S.S. St. Louis - 1939
Available in Kindle Only

The Crusades:
The Jewish World of the 12th Century
Available in Kindle Only

The Death of Berlin:
A Story of Hollocaust Survival and Revenge
Available in Kindle Only

The Remnant:
The Jewish Resistance in WWII
ISBN: 1519496346

The Uprising of Babi Yar:
The Syrets Deathcamp
Available in Kindle Only

Miscellaneous

Guaranteed Routes to Success for Writers:
A Road Map Through Today's
Dramatic Changes in Publishing
Available in Kindle Only

Joy of Volunteering:
Working and Surviving in Developing Countries
ISBN: 1519495587

So You Want to Write a Book:
ISBN: 1519496079

If you Found

So You Want
to Write a Book?

Helpful, Please leave a
review
on Amazon.com

Also availabel in Kindle

www.ingramcontent.com/pod-product-compliance
Lightning Source LLC
Chambersburg PA
CBHW071220280526
45787CB00002B/740